W9-BHI-715

COUNTRIES IN OUR WORLD

UNITED STATES
IN OUR WORLD

Lisa Klobuchar

Smart Apple Media

Published by Smart Apple Media
P.O. Box 3263, Mankato, Minnesota 56002

U.S. publication copyright © 2012 Smart Apple Media.
International copyright reserved in all countries. No
part of this book may be reproduced in any form
without written permission from the publisher.

Printed in the United States of America at Corporate
Graphics, in North Mankato, Minnesota.

Published by arrangement with the Watts Publishing
Group LTD, London.

Library of Congress Cataloging-in-Publication Data
Klobuchar, Lisa.
  United States in our world / by Lisa Klobuchar.
     p. cm. -- (Countries of the world)
  Summary: "Describes the geography, landscape,
economy, government, and culture of the United
States of America today and discusses the USA's
influence of and relations with the rest of the world"--
Provided by publisher.
  Includes index.
  ISBN 978-1-59920-436-9 (library binding)
  1. United States--Juvenile literature. I. Title.
  E156.K66 2012
  973--dc22
                              2010035509
1305
3-2011

9 8 7 6 5 4 3 2 1

Produced for Franklin Watts by
White-Thomson Publishing Ltd
Series consultant: Rob Bowden
Editor: Sonya Newland
Designer: Clare Nicholas
Picture researcher: Amy Sparks

Picture Credits
Corbis: 7 (Andrew Gombert/epa), 13 (Bettmann), 14
(Ed Kashi), 15 (Ed Kashi), 16 (Jeff Zelevansky/Reuters),
17 (John Gress/Reuters), 20 (Reuters), 23 (Steven
Georges/Press-Telegram), 25 (Matthew Cavanaugh/
epa), 28 (Guy Reynolds/Dallas Morning News).
Dreamstime: 4-5 (Michele Perbellini), 8 (Aliaksandr
Nikitsin), 9 (Ben Renard-Wiart), 10 (Elimitchell),
18–19 (Dreamshot); **FEMA News Photo:** 26 (Andrea
Booher); **iStock:** 29 (Jani Bryson); **NASA:** 21;
Shutterstock: 1 (Albert de Bruijn), 11 (Andy Z), 12
(Matt McClain), 19 (Byron W. Moore), 22 (Gary718),
24 (Albert de Bruijn), 27 (Christopher Halloran);
US Department of Defense: 6 (Edwin L. Wriston).

Contents

Introducing the United States

Its wealth and military might make the United States of America the most powerful country in the world. Despite criticism by other countries over economic problems and unpopular wars fought in the middle east, the United States still has a major influence on international economics and politics.

Where in the World?

Most of the United States lies in the middle part of the continent of North America. This is where 48 of the nation's 50 states are located. Two other states lie far away. Alaska is beyond the northwest border of Canada, the country to the north of the United States. Hawaii is made up of several islands in the South Pacific Ocean. Beyond the southernmost states lie Central and South America.

◀ *The Statue of Liberty is a symbol of freedom —one of the most treasured American values.*

IT'S A FACT!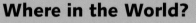

The Statue of Liberty commemorates the signing of the Declaration of Independence in 1776 when America began a campaign against British rule. A gift from France, the 150-foot (46 m) statue stands at the entrance to New York Harbor welcoming ships to "the land of the free."

Key
■ Capital city
○ Other cities

Hawaii

0   miles 150
0   150
kilometers

Alaska

0   miles 1000
0   1000
kilometers

CANADA

Seattle

ROCKY

GREAT PLAINS

□Yellowstone
National Park

Missouri River

GREAT LAKES

Boston

New York

Chicago

APPALACHIAN MOUNTAINS

■ Washington, DC

Jamestown

Pacific
Ocean

San Francisco

MOUNTAINS

UNITED
STATES

Grand Canyon □

Los Angeles

Mississippi River

Atlantic
Ocean

0   miles 300
0   300
kilometers

New Orleans

N

Gulf
of Mexico

W   E

Everglades □
National Park

Miami

MEXICO

S

A Young Nation

The United States was one of the first nations created when Europeans formed colonies overseas. About 400 years ago, people from Great Britain traveled across the ocean and first settled on the east coast of what is now the United States. In 1776, these settlers declared their independence from Britain, and after an eight-year war, the United States officially became an independent country.

▲ *The United States, the world's third-largest country, shares borders with Canada to the north and Mexico to the south.*

A Nation of Immigrants

Throughout its history, the United States has attracted settlers from all over the world. People moved there to seek opportunities and freedoms they did not have in their own countries. Its many immigrant communities have each left their own stamp on American life.

Global Superpower

After the collapse of the USSR in the 1990s, the United States emerged as the only superpower in the world. But what makes it so powerful? For one thing, it is the richest country in the world. The value of U.S. goods and services is almost twice that of China, which has the world's second-largest economy.

Military Strength

The United States also has the mightiest military

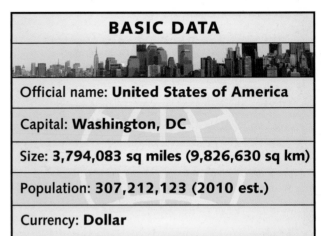

BASIC DATA
Official name: **United States of America**
Capital: **Washington, DC**
Size: **3,794,083 sq miles (9,826,630 sq km)**
Population: **307,212,123 (2010 est.)**
Currency: **Dollar**

in the world. It spends about 10 times more on its armed forces than China and Russia, which rank second and third. Despite this, China continues to grow in global power and influence, and will probably soon challenge the American status as the only superpower.

▼ *Although the war in Iraq is over, there is still a strong U.S. military presence there.*

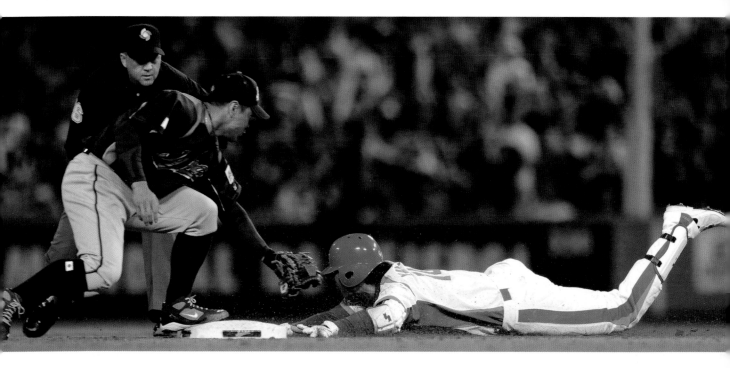

Troubled Times

The United States started a war in Iraq in 2003, believing that the Iraqis were hiding powerful weapons. The war itself lasted only a few weeks, but by 2010, about 50,000 American troops remained in Iraq. Although many countries supported the invasion of Iraq, others disagreed and many Americans protested against it also. In 2008, poor investments caused some large financial companies in the United States to fail. Many other countries were affected as a result, and a worldwide recession began.

Cultural Leader

One major way America makes its mark on the rest of the world is through its culture. American fast-food chains, such as McDonalds and Pizza Hut, thrive in many countries. American sports, such as baseball and basketball, have become popular throughout the world. People all over the globe enjoy, as well as mimic, American music, art, fashion, film, and television. However, not everyone appreciates America's influence on their countries' arts and culture. They feel that their own are lost as America's influence spreads.

▲ *American sports are enjoyed all over the world. Here, Japan and South Korea play in the final game of the 2009 World Baseball Classic.*

Landscapes and Environment

The United States covers the entire middle section of North America. It is the world's third-largest country—only Russia and Canada are larger. The United States stretches from the Pacific Ocean in the west to the Atlantic Ocean in the east. It shares a long border with Canada to the north and with Mexico to the south.

East of the Mississippi

The Mississippi River forms a dividing line between the different landscapes of the United States. East of the Mississippi lie the temperate forests of the Midwest and Northeast regions. In the far eastern part of the country is a region of highlands with several mountain ranges. The land slopes down to the east coast, which has many sandy beaches.

▼ *With a surface area of 31,820 sq miles (82,413 sq km), Lake Superior is a major waterway for transportation of goods, as well as a tourist destination.*

THE HOME OF...

The Great Lakes

The Great Lakes—five large freshwater lakes on the Canadian border in the north-central part of the United States—contain about 20 percent of the world's fresh water. The largest of the Great Lakes, Lake Superior, is the largest freshwater lake in the world.

West of the Mississippi

A huge, flat region lies in the middle part of the country. Part of this region is called the Great Plains, a fairly dry grassland where few trees grow. The towering Rocky Mountains run from Alaska to Mexico. To the west of the Rockies is a region of deserts, dry lowlands, and high plateaus. Mountain ranges and wide valleys make up the far western part of the country.

Climate

Most of the United States is in the earth's temperate middle latitudes. This means that it has cool or cold winters and warm or hot summers. But acoss the country there are many different climates. Scorching deserts lie in the southwest. In the northwest are cool, rainy forests. Alaska has an arctic climate with bitterly cold winters and short, cool summers. Hawaii and Florida have a tropical climate with warm temperatures all year.

▼ *Southwestern United States is hot and dry. Here, in the desert of Utah, the wind has worn the sandstone into shapes such as pillars and arches.*

IT'S A FACT!

Hurricane Katrina struck the Gulf Coast in August 2005, destroying parts of the historic city of New Orleans in Louisiana, as well as damaging other coastal cities in Mississippi and Alabama. About 1,300 people died as a result of the storm, and it caused an estimated $125 billion in damage. In terms of economic damage, Katrina was the worst natural disaster in U.S. history.

Protecting Wildlife

The United States has hundreds of national parks and refuges where the environment and wildlife are protected. The largest refuge is the 31,250 sq mile (81,000 sq km) Yukon Delta National Wildlife Refuge in Alaska. In 2002 and 2003, President George W. Bush tried to pass laws that would allow oil companies to drill in the Alaskan Arctic National Wildlife Refuge. Many people were afraid of the damage this would do to the environment. The refuge is home to grizzly bears, caribou, polar bears, and many types of birds and fish. In the end, the laws were not passed.

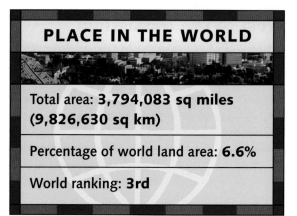

PLACE IN THE WORLD

Total area: **3,794,083 sq miles (9,826,630 sq km)**

Percentage of world land area: **6.6%**

World ranking: **3rd**

▼ *Animals such as caribou make their homes in freezing Alaska. The country's largest national parks lie in this relatively unpopulated area.*

▲ *In some big cities, such as Los Angeles, air pollution is so bad that a permanent smog hangs over.*

Controlling Pollution

The United States faces many environmental challenges. Pollution from factories, farms, and cars endangers people's health and the environment. The Environmental Protection Agency (EPA) sets pollution rules, but the United States is still the world's worst polluter and the biggest generator of waste. The U.S. government has passed laws to control pollution, such as the Clean Air Act and the Clean Water Act.

IT STARTED HERE

Earth Day

Earth Day is a special day to make people aware of the environmental issues threatening our planet. It was first celebrated on April 22, 1970, after U.S. Senator Gaylord Nelson organized a protest against how little was being done to protect the environment. Earth Day is now celebrated all over the world every year.

Population and Migration

Many people call the United States a "melting pot." This means that immigrants from all over the world have incorporated their unique traditions and beliefs, which have influenced American culture today.

Colonial Life

The first people to live in what is now the United States were Native Americans. They belonged to many different groups, each with its own traditions and beliefs. Beginning in the late 1500s, settlers from European countries began to arrive. From about 1600 to 1750, Europeans settled throughout the eastern part of present-day America. Most of them were from England, so the new land became a British colony. The population also included people from the Netherlands, France, Sweden, Germany, and most other Western European countries. Some Africans were brought against their will and put to work as slaves. Descendants of all these people contribute to the American population today.

Moving Westwards

The United States of America was born after the colonists won a war of independence against Britain in 1783. The new country grew steadily over the next 100 years. In 1803, President Thomas Jefferson bought a huge piece of land in the middle of the country from France, which doubled the size of America.

◀ *This statue in Jamestown, Virginia, commemorates Captain John Smith who helped establish the first permanent English settlement in America.*

People began traveling west into lands that had previously been unexplored by Europeans. The U.S. government gave away land on the prairies to people who would farm it. These people were known as homesteaders. The Native Americans, who had once moved freely across these lands, were forced onto controlled areas called reservations.

Waves of Immigration

Throughout its history, the United States has welcomed millions of immigrants. From 1820 to 1870, about 7.5 million people arrived, many of them from Ireland and Germany. Then, from 1870 to 1916, about 25 million more people arrived, doubling its population. Most of them were from Eastern Europe and China.

FAMOUS AMERICAN

Jane Addams (1860–1935)

Jane Addams devoted her life to helping immigrants and the poor in America. She founded Hull House in Chicago in 1889. There, immigrants learned the skills they needed to become American citizens. Addams won the Nobel Peace Prize in 1931.

▼ *Immigrants arriving in America in the early 20th century.*

The Population Today

In 1960, 83 percent of Americans were white people who were born there. Most of the rest were black Americans descended from African slaves. By 2006, only 67 percent of Americans were native-born whites. About 14 percent were Hispanic (from the Spanish-speaking countries of Central America) and 12 percent were black. About 12 percent of the U.S. population were immigrants. This most recent wave of immigration is still going on today.

PLACE IN THE WORLD

Population: 307,212,123 (2010 est.)

Percentage of world total: 4.5%

World ranking: 3rd

Where Do Americans Live?

The coastal regions along the Atlantic and Pacific oceans and the Gulf of Mexico are home to about 38 percent of Americans. About 33 percent live around the Great Lakes and in the Northeast region. Most of the rest live in the Rocky Mountain and Great Plains states. The area between Boston, Massachusetts, and Washington, DC, is the most densely populated.

▼ *Hispanic immigrant workers from Latin America pick beans in a field in Florida. This group makes up the latest wave of U.S. immigrants.*

Americans on the Move

Americans as a group relocate more than people in the rest of the world. The average American moves 11 to 13 times in his or her life, mostly within the United States, but sometimes abroad. As different parts of the United States are made up of people from different ethnic backgrounds, such a mobile population helps Americans become familiar with different cultures. It also helps create the multicultural society that is typical in America.

▲ *America is one of the most multicultural countries in the world with people from many ethnic backgrounds.*

Standard of Living

Americans enjoy one of the highest standards of living in the world. But in some ways the United States does not meet the same standards as other developed countries. It has a higher divorce rate, lower educational performance, higher rates of crime and homelessness, and a higher infant mortality rate than many countries in Western Europe.

GLOBAL LEADER

Immigration

The United States leads the world in immigration. In 2007, most newcomers came from Mexico, China, the Philippines, India, and El Salvador. Almost one-third of the foreign-born people in the U.S. were from Mexico.

15

Culture and Lifestyles

American fast food, pop music, TV shows, movies, and clothing styles have spread across the globe. They influence the culture and lifestyles of millions of people.

Freedom to be Different

The American people have a strong sense of shared culture. Most Americans speak English and have similar habits of dress, food, and housing. At the same time, descendants from the different groups of early settlers are often proud of their individual heritage. The traditions of many countries, have blended to create American culture. This makes Americans more tolerant than people in many other countries, and gives them a strong belief in equality and freedom.

Personal Space

Americans are unique among other Western cultures in their desire to live apart from others. Most Americans prefer to live in suburbs rather than in crowded cities.

▶ *As suburbs grew, shopping malls became popular as a way for people to get everything they needed at one stop.*

IT STARTED HERE

Shopping Malls

The first modern enclosed shopping mall was built in Edina, Minnesota in 1956. It was the first mall to be built on more than one level and entirely enclosed. It became the model for nearly all shopping malls today.

The American Dream

Since the mid-1900s, the typical "American dream" has been to own a large house in the suburbs with at least one car. After the end of World War II in 1945, there was a large movement of people leaving the big cities to relocate in the suburbs. This was largely because there was the available space to spread out—the United States is a large country and had not been settled for hundreds of years like many other countries.

A Religious Nation

In America people are free to follow any religion they want. Surveys show that about 7 in 10 Americans believe in God, and around half of them say that religion is very important in their lives. More than 80 percent of Americans call themselves Christians, although not all of them are practicing.

IT'S A FACT!

Christian congregations in America have grown bigger over the last 20 years. A megachurch is a Christian church with more than 2,000 members. Services usually feature live music and videos projected on large screens. In 2008, there were about 1,360 megachurches in the United States. About 5 million people attend services at megachurches across America each week.

▼ *This megachurch in Illinois can seat 7,000 people. Big screens allow everyone to see the preacher and to share in the experience.*

Festivals and Celebrations

One of the most important national holidays in the United States is Independence Day. Every year on July 4, Americans celebrate the adoption of the Declaration of Independence and freedom from British rule. Families and friends have picnics, and there are often local fireworks displays. Thanksgiving is a harvest festival celebrated in November to commemorate the help the Native Americans gave the early settlers by sharing food.

GOING GLOBAL

Fast food, which started in America, has exploded around the world. McDonald's has 30,000 restaurants worldwide in 119 countries. KFC, the fried chicken chain, is especially popular in China, where it operates 800 restaurants.

A Sporting Nation

Americans are huge sports fans and therefore sports are an important part of American culture. The most popular sports are football, baseball, basketball, and ice hockey, and the United States leads the world in these sports. Americans support their teams passionately. Championship games such as football's Super Bowl and baseball's World Series attract thousands of fans to the live event and millions more who watch on TV. Soccer—the most popular sport in the world—is not nearly as popular as other sports in the U.S.

▼ *Crowds in the National Mall park in Washington, DC, celebrate Independence Day on July 4. Families gather for picnics and to watch fireworks after the sun sets.*

Film and Music

The films, TV, and musical styles that make up American pop culture are the most famous U.S. exports. As the home of Hollywood, America has influenced the film industry in many other countries, but it is also known for creating TV dramas that are popular all over the world. Musical genres such as jazz, blues, and country music were all born in America. Later, these were developed into modern styles such as rock 'n' roll, rap, soul, and funk. Today, American film and pop stars are sometimes known across the globe, and are more famous than native stars in many countries.

THE HOME OF...

Hollywood

The area of Los Angeles known as Hollywood is the heart of the world's film industry. The first film studio was set up there in 1909, and since then, Hollywood has set the standard for blockbuster movies all over the world, making and releasing hundreds of films every year. Its influence is so widespread that the Indian film industry based in Mumbai has been nicknamed "Bollywood."

Economy and Trade

The United States has by far the largest economy in the world. The country is rich in resources, including fertile farmland, waterways, minerals, and forests. In 2008, it produced about US$15 billion worth of goods and services. But hard times struck and the U.S. suffered a recession, which spread around the world.

Free Enterprise

The economy of the United States is based on free enterprise. This means that the people, rather than the government, manage the economy. The government makes some rules and laws, and controls some business activities to make sure that businesses operate fairly. This helps ensure Americans get the goods and services they need. However, the people decide what to make, how to make it, what to sell, and for how much money.

▼ *Bill Gates—one of the richest men in the world—shows off Microsoft's Tablet PC.*

FAMOUS AMERICAN

Bill Gates
(b. 1955)

Bill Gates is a pioneer in the personal-computer industry. With a boyhood friend, Paul Allen, he founded Microsoft in 1975. They developed operating systems—programs that tell computers how to run. Today, Microsoft is the world's largest software company, selling the world's top operating system, Windows.

Growing Service Industries

As in other Western countries, the American service industry employs most of the workers and creates most of the country's wealth. Service industries are those that provide services for people rather than making products. In the early 2000s, 83 percent of America's workers were employed in service industries, such as real estate, tourism, healthcare, hotels, law firms, banking, and restaurants.

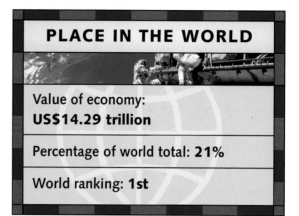

PLACE IN THE WORLD

Value of economy:
US$14.29 trillion

Percentage of world total: **21%**

World ranking: **1st**

High-tech Leader

The United States has long been known as a leader in technology, and this brings a lot of money into the economy. For the most part, it has led the world in advances in computers, medicine, spacecraft, air travel, and military equipment. In particular, it led the way in space technology. America was the first country to put a man on the Moon, and it now plays an important part in the International Space Station (ISS), a joint project among the United States, Russia, Japan, Canada, and countries of the European Space Agency.

▼ *An American astronaut and one from the European Space Agency work on the International Space Station.*

Global Economy

The United States is both the world's biggest importer and the world's biggest exporter of goods and services. Recently, however, the U.S. economy has become more dependent on the goods and services of other countries. For example, U.S. companies import car parts from other countries. The vehicles are put together in the United States, and the finished products are then shipped abroad to be sold. America's top trading partners in 2008 were Canada, China, Mexico, Japan, and Germany.

▲ *The Port of Miami is one of the largest in the United States. Both container ships for importing and exporting goods and cruise ships use this port.*

Manufacturing

Businesses that produce goods such as steel, cars, computers, toys, and clothing are called manufacturers. The United States is the world leader in manufacturing, and American products—from Apple iPods to Disney merchandise—can be found everywhere. However, there are now fewer workers in the manufacturing industry than ever before. Over the past 30 years, many American companies have built factories in other countries, such as China, Mexico, and India, where labor costs are lower. This means that many American manufacturing jobs have been lost.

GOING GLOBAL

American children play with mostly foreign-made toys. Almost 90 percent of all toys sold in the U.S. are imported, and China supplies more than three-quarters of them.

The Tourist Industry

Tourism is big business in the United States. In fact, America earns more from tourists than any other country in the world. In 2007, tourism brought nearly US$98 billion into the U.S. economy. Because the United States is such a large country, it has many different attractions for tourists. Some come to enjoy the sunshine and beaches in places like California, or to go to amusement parks like Disneyland. Others visit the many national parks and natural sites like the Grand Canyon. Still others visit big cities such as New York to see the museums and galleries, or just to enjoy the shopping.

▼ *Disneyland in California is one of the world's top tourist attraction, with about 15 million visitors per year.*

Economic Hard Times

In 2007, the U.S. economy seemed strong, but there were signs of trouble. Prices for necessities such as healthcare and gasoline were rising, but people's wages were not. By late 2008, many businesses, including major banks and car companies, had failed. People started to compare this economic crisis to the Great Depression—a period of severe economic hardship that lasted from the late 1920s to the late 1930s. In 2008 and early 2009, the U.S. government spent more than US$1.2 trillion to rescue troubled companies and create projects to employ people.

Government and Politics

The United States was formed a little more than 230 years ago, but its constitution—the document that describes the basic principles of how the country will be run—is the oldest written constitution still in use. It has lasted such a long time because it has ensured a stable government and a good life for most Americans.

Power from the People

According to the constitution, the power is held by the people of America. It states clearly what powers the government has, which include the authority to collect taxes, to maintain the armed forces, and to carry on trade with other countries. The constitution also limits the power of the government by granting American citizens certain rights. For example, the government cannot tell people what religion they must follow or punish people for what they say or write publicly.

THE HOME OF...

The White House

The White House is the home and official workplace of the U.S. president. It is in Washington, DC, and was built between 1792 and 1800. Not far from the White House is the United States Capitol, which is where Congress—the Senate and the House of Representatives—meets.

▼ *The White House has become a global symbol of democracy.*

Federal System

The United States has a federal system of government. This means that the country is made up of separate states united under the federal, or national, government. Each state can make its own laws on matters such as education or punishments for crimes, but state laws cannot conflict with laws passed by the federal government—and all laws must follow the rules of the constitution.

Three Branches of Government

The U.S. government is made up of three branches: executive, legislative, and judicial. The president of the United States is the leader of the executive branch, which carries out the laws. Two groups of lawmakers—the House of Representatives and the Senate—make up the legislative branch. They write and pass new laws. The judicial branch is made up of courts led by judges. The judicial branch settles disagreements about laws. It also decides whether laws passed by the House and Senate follow the rules of the U.S. constitution. Each branch of the government can undo actions by the other branches, which makes sure that no one branch can grow too powerful.

▲ *The United States Congress is jointly made up of the House of Representatives and the Senate. The men and women of Congress are elected by the people in their home state.*

World Superpower

America's position as the world's only superpower means that it has a lot of influence over international affairs. Other countries will often follow America's lead in matters of war, international politics, and economic policy. Decisions made in the United States can have a far-reaching effect. The power the United States has makes it a model for other nations, but it also can make it a target for criticism.

Terrorist Attacks

On September 11, 2001, Islamic terrorists destroyed the World Trade Center, two large office towers in New York City. In response to this, the U.S. government declared a "War on Terror," determined to catch the people who had carried out the attacks and prevent such an event from happening again.

GOING GLOBAL

The U.S. government suspected that Iraq was involved in the terrorist attacks and claimed that the country had weapons of mass destruction. U.S. troops invaded Iraq in 2003 and overthrew its leader, Saddam Hussein. The UK, Australia, Poland, and Denmark also sent troops to Iraq, but countries such as France, Germany, and Russia were against the invasion.

▲ *Firefighters search through the rubble after the 9/11 terrorist attacks in New York.*

The War on Terror

To prevent another terrorist attack on U.S. soil, the government took drastic measures. It passed laws making it legal to spy on Americans. It started wars in Iraq and Afghanistan, where Islamic terrorists were believed to be. It also imprisoned many suspected terrorists in a prison camp at Guantanamo Bay in Cuba.

Promising Change

When Barack Obama became president in January 2009, he promised to change many policies that Americans were unhappy with. In particular, he announced that he would begin bringing the troops home from Iraq. He ordered the release of records proving that the United States government had previously carried out widespread torture of prisoners. President Obama also promised to close the prison at Guantanamo Bay. He made visits to the Middle East in an effort to improve relations with the Islamic world.

FAMOUS AMERICAN

Barack Obama (b. 1961)

Barack Obama, the son of an American mother and a Kenyan father, grew up in Hawaii and Indonesia. He entered politics in 1996 when he was elected to the Illinois Senate, and in 2005 he became a U.S. senator. In January 2009, he became the U.S. president—the first African-American to hold that position.

▶ *Many Americans felt that President Barack Obama's election was a turning point for the country, and that the political and economic situation would begin to improve.*

It is likely that the United States will continue to be the world's most powerful nation for some years, despite the rise of China as a global power. Throughout the next few years, living standards in America may improve, and standards in other countries may become more equal to U.S. standards. The U.S. population will also change as immigration rises and the birth rate slows.

Changing Face of the Nation

In 2010, about 12 percent of the U.S. population was foreign-born. By 2050, that number is expected to rise to 19 percent. It is estimated that 67 million people will immigrate to the U.S. in the next 40 years. By 2020, it is thought that the number of children of foreign-born Hispanics will have doubled from what it was in 2000. These people may not have equal education and job opportunities compared with other groups, so the gap between rich and poor may grow wider.

▼ *Immigrant children hold up the certificates that prove they are now American citizens.*

Population Growth

Unlike many developed countries in Europe and Asia where populations are declining, the population of the United States is still growing. People are also living longer, and in coming years, the number of senior citizens will grow. By 2020, the U.S. Census Bureau expects that about one in every five people will be 65 or older. There will be fewer younger workers creating wealth, so the United States will be challenged to find ways to care for its aging population. More older Americans will also be working well beyond today's retirement age of 65.

The Future of Trade

Most experts believe that all over the world trade among different countries will go up. The U.S. will continue to be a part of that growth. In 2007, imports made up about 17 percent of the total U.S. economy. Exports of U.S. products were about 12 percent. The U.S. government believes that by 2027, these numbers will rise dramatically, and imports will be about 26 percent of the U.S. economy and exports will be about 27 percent.

▲ *Schoolchildren say the Pledge of Allegiance in front of the U.S. flag. People under the age of 20 currently make up one quarter of the U.S. population, but that balance is expected to shift in the near future.*

Glossary

Christianity a religion that follows the teachings of Jesus Christ.

colony a territory under the immediate political control of a nation.

conservation protecting and preserving the natural environment and wildlife.

constitution a document that lays out the main laws of a nation; laws are not allowed to be passed that contradict a country's constitution.

continent one of the earth's seven great land masses; Africa, Antarctica, Asia, Australia, Europe, North America, and South America are continents.

democracy a form of government in which people vote for the leaders they wish to represent them.

economy the financial system of a country or region, including how much money is made from the production and sale of goods and services.

ethnic group a group of people who identify with each other and feel they share a history.

export to transport products or materials abroad for sale or trade.

immigrant a person who has moved to another country to live.

import to bring in goods or materials from a foreign country for sale.

infant mortality the number of children who die before reaching adulthood in a particular country.

minerals natural rocks that come from the ground.

plateau an area of high, flat land.

pollution ruining the environment with man-made waste, such as gases from vehicle emissions or chemicals from factories or pesticides.

prairie a large expanse of grassland, where few trees grow.

recession an extended period when the economy of a country slows down.

reservations special areas of land set aside for the Native American people after they were driven off their native land by white settlers.

resources things that are available to use, often to help develop a country's industry and economy; resources could be minerals, workers (labor), water, or many other things.

suburbs areas on the outskirts of cities that are less built-up than city centers.

terrorist a person who uses violence or causes fear to try to change a political system or policy.

USSR Union of Soviet Socialist Republics; a communist country in eastern Europe and northern Asia, in 1991, the USSR split into independent countries, including Russia.

Further Information

Books

The United States
Welcome to My Country
by Nicole Frank and Elizabeth Berg
(Marshall Cavendish, 2011)

United States of America
Enchantment of the World
by Michael Burgan
(Children's Press, 2008)

United States
Celebrate!
by Robyn Hardyman
(Chelsea Clubhouse, 2009)

Web Sites

**http://www.americaslibrary.gov/cgi-bin/
page.cgi**
The Library of Congress site with information for kids
about American people, states, and historical events.

**http://www.travelforkids.com/Funtodo/United_States
/usa.htm**
Take a journey through the U.S. with this fun site,
traveling from Alaska to Hawaii.

hhttp://bensguide.gpo.gov/index.html
With Ben Franklin as a guide, learn about the three
branches of the U.S. government.

*Every effort has been made by the publisher to ensure
that these web sites contain no inappropriate or offensive
material. However, because of the nature of the Internet,
it is impossible to guarantee that the content of these sites
will not be altered. We strongly advise that Internet access
is supervised by a responsible adult.*

Index

Numbers in **bold** indicate pictures